# From click to art a journey through photography

Robin Hjertqvist

Published by Robin Hjertqvist, 2024.

FROM CLICK TO ART A JOURNEY THROUGH PHOTOGRAPHY

**First edition. October 30, 2024.**

Copyright © 2024 Robin Hjertqvist.

ISBN: 979-8227523341

Written by Robin Hjertqvist.

# Welcome to My World of Photography

Welcome to my book about photography! I'm genuinely glad you're here, and I hope you find inspiration and valuable insights that will help you elevate your photographic skills.

My name is Robin Hjertqvist , and my journey as a photographer began a few years ago when I felt an irresistible urge to capture moments and tell stories through images. My grandfather had a passion for photography, and after seeing his incredible pictures, I was inspired to pick up a camera myself. I have always been captivated by how a single image can encapsulate a feeling, a moment, or a cherished memory. Observing how light dances across surfaces, how colors interact, and how people connect is an ever-evolving art form that continuously fascinates me.

I became particularly drawn to street photography, a genre that allows me to dive into the vibrant tapestry of everyday life in various cities across Sweden. Wandering with my camera in hand gives me a sense of freedom and adventure. Each street and corner has its own story waiting to be told. Capturing a fleeting glance between two strangers, children playing in the street, or an elderly man sitting on a bench, watching life unfold—these moments are small treasures filled with authentic emotions and events. Street photography provides a unique opportunity to see the world in its purest form, beyond the posed images of weddings or portraits. It is in these unguarded moments that I find my inspiration and a deeper understanding of human life.

On my journeys, I've been fortunate to visit several cities within my country, capturing everything from bustling urban streets to quieter, more secluded spots. Each location boasts its own culture, colors, and moods, and it's an honor for me to immortalize these moments through my lens. Street photography is not merely about capturing images; it's about capturing the soul of a moment. By sharing these photographs, I hope to inspire others to view the world through the same lens and discover the beauty in the everyday.

In this book, I share my experiences, tips, and tricks I've gathered over the years. I will also provide recommendations for equipment and where to find quality, affordable photography gear that fits your budget. My goal is to help you grow as a photographer and capture your own memories meaningfully.

This book is crafted with amateur photographers and hobbyists in mind, as well as anyone genuinely interested in photography. I want you to feel empowered to pick up your camera and venture into the world with curiosity and courage. Whether you're a beginner or have some experience, I hope my insights and stories will provide the motivation you need to explore and enhance your photography.

Thank you for choosing to read my book. I look forward to sharing this journey with you and hope it inspires you to go out and capture life's beautiful moments—perhaps even discovering a new passion for street photography along the way. Let's embark on this journey together, and may you find joy and inspiration in every picture you take.

**Basic Settings: The Key to Great Photos**

For me, the basic camera settings are like keys that unlock creativity. When I first started with photography, understanding all the settings and technical terms felt overwhelming. But the more I learned, the more I realized that these settings—aperture, shutter speed, and ISO—are not just technical choices; they're tools that allow me to capture moments in exactly the way I want. They let me create images that feel alive, that tell a story and convey an emotion. So let me walk you through these three essential settings and how I use them in my own photography.

**Aperture: Creating Depth and Focus**

I like to think of the aperture as the "eyelid" of the camera. Imagine that when the eyelid opens wide (a small f-number), a lot of light floods in, perfect for low-light conditions or creating a beautifully blurred background that makes the subject stand out. This is a technique I often use in portraits or when I want to focus on a particular detail in the image. A large aperture creates a soft background, almost dreamlike, and automatically draws the viewer's attention to the most important part of the photo.

On the other hand, when I use a small aperture (a large f-number), I let in less light, but I get greater depth of field across the image. This is fantastic for landscapes or street scenes where I want every detail to be crisp and sharp, from the foreground to the horizon. With a small aperture, it feels like I can freeze an entire scene in time, inviting the viewer to take in every tiny part of what I saw through the lens.

So, aperture isn't just about light; it's about creating depth and focus. Choosing the right aperture for the right moment is like deciding which "chapter" of the photo is going to tell the story.


**Shutter Speed: Freezing or Blurring Motion**

When it comes to shutter speed, I think of it as how long the camera's "eye" stays open to take in the world. A fast shutter speed, like 1/1000th of a second, is like blinking quickly—it freezes motion, allowing me to capture a moment in perfect detail, like a dog running or someone jumping in the air. The power of a fast shutter speed is that it stops time, and there's a pure joy in capturing movement in a way that our eyes might miss in real life.

But when I slow down the shutter speed, say to 1/30th of a second, I open up the possibility to capture motion in the image, which creates a dreamlike feeling. It could be the flow of a streaming river or people moving down a busy street. With a slower shutter speed, I can add a sense of softness and flow, almost like the photo is breathing. This is something I love to use when I want to convey a sense of life and energy in the image, as if the viewer is pulled into the motion.

For me, shutter speed is more than just a technical setting; it's a tool to control time and movement, to let the viewer experience a moment as I saw it—either frozen in time or with a hint of fleeting motion.

### ISO: Sensitivity to Light

ISO is the camera's sensitivity to light, and I think of it as the camera's "eyes" adjusting depending on how dark or bright it is. A low ISO, like 100, gives the clearest, sharpest images, which is ideal in daylight or brightly lit environments. When I use a high ISO, like 800 or above, I can capture subjects even in darker settings. But I'm always mindful that the higher the ISO, the more "grainy" the image can become, which can sometimes take away from the detail.

Finding the right balance with ISO is often about weighing how much light is available and the atmosphere I want to create. I see it as a way to adapt the camera to the environment and mood. Sometimes it's worth increasing the ISO to capture that raw feeling, while other times, a clear and sharp image is more important. Mastering ISO gives me the freedom to shoot no matter the lighting conditions and to create the right mood in each photo.

## Composition: Telling a Story with Images

Now that we've gone through the basic settings, let's dive into the world of composition. If the settings are the "language," then composition is the story itself. By thinking about how I place different elements within the frame, I can guide how the viewer perceives the scene and what they're drawn to first. It's through composition that I can truly tell a story with each image.

### Rule of Thirds: Balancing Elements

One of the most valuable techniques for me is the Rule of Thirds. I imagine dividing the image into three equal parts, both horizontally and vertically, creating a grid. By placing the most important elements where the lines intersect, I create a more balanced and interesting image. The Rule of Thirds helps guide the viewer's eye through the photo in a natural way, and it often feels like the image gains a harmony that wouldn't exist if the subject was placed directly in the center.

For example, when I take a portrait, I often place the person slightly to the left or right of the center, which draws the eye to them first. For landscapes, I can use the Rule of Thirds to balance the sky and the ground, giving a sense of depth and perspective. It's a simple rule, but it can make a big difference in how a photo feels to the viewer.

### Composition: Telling a Story with Images

Once I understood the basics of camera settings, I quickly realized that composition is where the magic truly happens. Composition isn't just about placing subjects within the frame; it's about weaving a story, creating a visual journey, and inviting the viewer to see the world through my eyes. Through composition, I can convey emotions, highlight beauty, and guide the viewer's focus. Let me share some of my favorite composition techniques and how they've helped me tell more compelling stories with my images.

### Rule of Thirds: Balancing Elements and Adding Interest

One of the first techniques I learned in photography, and one that I return to time and time again, is the Rule of Thirds. Imagine dividing your image into three equal parts, both horizontally and vertically, creating a grid with nine sections. By placing key elements along these lines or at their intersections, I create a more balanced and engaging image. The Rule of Thirds adds a natural flow, guiding the viewer's eye in a way that feels almost effortless.

For example, when I'm photographing a person, I rarely place them dead center. Instead, I might position them slightly to the left or right, aligning their eyes or their face along one of the vertical lines. This creates a more dynamic image, one that feels balanced yet interesting, as if inviting the viewer to explore beyond the subject.

When I shoot landscapes, I often use the Rule of Thirds to balance the horizon. Placing the horizon either in the top third or bottom third of the frame helps to emphasize either the sky or the foreground, depending on which part I want to highlight. It's a subtle shift, but it brings a whole new depth to the scene, making the viewer feel as though they're standing right there with me.

**Leading Lines: Guiding the Viewer's Eye**

Leading lines are one of my favorite tools to use in composition, especially in urban or street photography. These lines could be anything—roads, fences, shadows, rivers—that naturally lead the eye through the image toward the subject. It's like giving the viewer a path to follow, drawing them into the story of the photo.

In a busy cityscape, a road or pathway can serve as a strong leading line, guiding the viewer's gaze from the foreground to the background, revealing details gradually. Leading lines add depth and a sense of movement, as if the viewer is journeying through the photo alongside me. When I find a powerful leading line, it feels like discovering a hidden route that unlocks the story of the image.

Sometimes, these lines don't just lead to the main subject but create a frame within the frame, adding layers to the image. I love how leading lines can transform a simple composition into something captivating, drawing the viewer in and making them feel connected to the scene.

**Framing: Creating Depth and Focus**

Framing is another technique that I find incredibly powerful. By using elements within the scene—like tree branches, doorways, or windows—as natural frames around my subject, I can create a sense of focus and isolation. It's as if I'm inviting the viewer to take a closer look at what I want them to see, saying, "Look here; this is important."

I remember one shot where I used an archway to frame a bustling street scene. The arch not only directed attention to the activity in the center but also added a sense of intimacy, as though the viewer was peeking into a private moment of daily life. Framing can also add context, giving a hint of the surroundings without taking focus away from the main subject. It's a technique I return to often, as it allows me to create depth and layers within a single image.

**Symmetry and Patterns: Finding Harmony and Rhythm**

Symmetry and patterns are natural forms of beauty that I'm always drawn to. There's something deeply satisfying about capturing an image where the elements are perfectly balanced or where a pattern repeats itself, creating a rhythm within the frame. Symmetry brings a sense of order, while patterns provide visual interest, pulling the viewer in to explore the details.

In urban environments, I often find symmetry in architecture—rows of windows, lines of streetlights, or reflections in glass buildings. Nature, too, is full of symmetry and patterns, whether it's the petals of a flower or the ripples on a pond. Whenever I spot these repeating shapes or lines, I feel compelled to capture them. It's as if they create a visual rhythm that makes the image feel calm and cohesive.

Sometimes, I like to break the symmetry intentionally. By introducing an element that disrupts the pattern—a person walking through a row of identical columns, for example—I can create a focal point that immediately draws the eye. This contrast between order and surprise keeps the viewer engaged, making the image feel both familiar and unique.

**Negative Space: Embracing Simplicity**

Negative space, or the empty areas surrounding the subject, is a technique I often use to emphasize simplicity and focus. By allowing space around my subject, I create a sense of calm and clarity, letting the main element of the photo stand out without distractions. Negative space is like breathing room for the eyes, inviting the viewer to pause and take in the details.

I remember capturing a lone bird flying across an expansive sky, with nothing but clouds around it. By leaving a lot of empty space, I was able to convey a feeling of solitude and freedom. Negative space adds a sense of minimalism, encouraging the viewer to focus on what's there rather than what's missing. It's a reminder that sometimes, less is more, and that a simple composition can be just as powerful as a complex one.

Using negative space also allows me to play with the mood of the image. When I want to evoke a sense of loneliness or peacefulness, I often rely on negative space to let the emotions breathe. It's a technique that I find both challenging and rewarding, as it requires a careful balance between emptiness and focus.

**Macro Photography: Discovering the World in Tiny Details**

Macro photography is like stepping into a hidden world, a personal invitation to explore the intricate beauty that often goes unnoticed. It's an intimate journey where even the smallest subjects become grand landscapes of patterns and textures. Getting close enough to capture the delicate veins on a leaf or the mesmerizing, detailed structure of an insect's wing feels like uncovering a hidden treasure. Each click of the shutter is an adventure, an exploration of beauty that the naked eye would likely overlook.

One of the first things I learned in macro photography was the importance of stability. Using a tripod became essential, especially when capturing these tiny details where even the slightest shake can blur the shot. With a steady setup, I can experiment with angles, lighting, and depth in a way that brings out the true essence of these tiny worlds. I find myself trying different perspectives, sometimes lying on the ground or positioning the camera in unusual angles, and each attempt often leads to surprising compositions that I never could have imagined.

Patience is key in macro photography. It requires waiting for the wind to settle, adjusting the light just right, and sometimes taking countless shots to capture a single, perfect image. But each challenge feels worthwhile. When I finally capture a sharp, detailed image of a flower petal's edge or the textures on a bug's back, it feels as though I've unlocked a secret that nature was keeping.

In this process, I've developed a deeper appreciation for the world around me. It's remarkable how much beauty exists in places we rarely take the time to notice. With every close-up shot, I find myself in awe of nature's complexity and design. Each tiny world I photograph reminds me to look closer and appreciate the small wonders that surround us every day.

**Street Photography: Capturing Life in Its Rawest Form**

Street photography holds a special place in my heart because it's not just about taking photos—it's about capturing life as it unfolds, raw and unscripted. There's a thrill in blending into the crowd, becoming invisible, and watching moments play out naturally. I love the feeling of being a silent observer, witnessing genuine expressions and interactions without interrupting the flow of the scene. It's in these candid moments, the ones people often overlook, that the most authentic stories come to life.

Each photograph tells its own story, whether it's a fleeting glance shared between strangers, a child's laughter echoing down a narrow alley, or a street performer lost in their art. These little slices of life make me appreciate the beauty in the ordinary, and it's this authenticity that keeps me coming back to street photography. I want my photos to feel like time capsules, preserving a small piece of the city's life and energy for others to experience.

Street photography also teaches me patience and observation. I never know what I'll find or where the next interesting moment will happen, and that unpredictability is part of the excitement. Sometimes I'll walk for hours, exploring new streets and waiting for a scene that captures the essence of a place or the spirit of the people there. It's about being present, noticing the subtleties, and finding beauty in the mundane.

For me, every street photo is a little story, a fragment of life that might otherwise go unnoticed. It's a way of connecting with the world and capturing moments that reveal the heart of a city, the soul of its people, and the quiet poetry of everyday life.

**Wedding Photography: Preserving Memories for a Lifetime**

Weddings are so much more than ceremonies—they're vibrant tapestries woven with emotions, stories, and fleeting moments that deserve to be cherished forever. To me, wedding photography is about storytelling. My goal is to document not just the big moments, like the vows and the first dance, but also the smaller, intimate ones—the joyful tears, the quiet smiles, the quick, loving glances shared between the couple. These are the memories that will live on, and I feel an immense responsibility in capturing them.

I pay close attention to details, from the rings to the decorations, to help tell the full story of the day. Communication with the couple is key; I like to meet with them beforehand to understand their vision and what's most meaningful to them. This way, when the big day arrives, I can blend into the background and let the moments unfold naturally. It's about being there without being intrusive, capturing the day as it happens without interrupting the flow of events.

For me, wedding photography is about more than just beautiful images; it's about preserving memories that will be cherished for generations. Knowing that these photos will be looked at time and time again, bringing the couple back to the emotions of their day, is a privilege I don't take lightly. I want my images to have that timeless quality, to make the couple feel like they're reliving their wedding day every time they look at their album.

In the end, capturing a wedding feels like capturing the beginning of a new story, one that I'm honored to be a small part of. It's a role that comes with responsibility and joy, and it's one of the most rewarding aspects of my work as a photographer.

**Event Photography: Immersing in the Atmosphere**

Event photography is all about capturing the energy, excitement, and emotions of a gathering, whether it's a lively concert, a colorful festival, or a corporate celebration. Every event has its unique vibe, and my goal is to document not just the people but the entire atmosphere. The energy in the air is often palpable, and I strive to create a visual story that allows viewers to feel as if they were there, immersed in the experience.

Event photography requires me to be quick on my feet and adaptable, ready to adjust to changing lighting conditions and the unpredictable flow of the event. There's often no second chance to capture a moment, so staying alert is crucial. I enjoy the challenge of reading the room, sensing where the action will be, and framing each shot to reflect the event's mood and energy. It's like piecing together a visual narrative, from the dramatic stage lights casting shadows to the candid shots of people laughing and enjoying themselves.

For me, every event has its own character, and it's a thrill to be the one capturing it for others to relive. I see my role as a storyteller, documenting not just the highlights but also the small moments that give the event its unique feel. Each event I photograph adds a new chapter to my journey as a photographer, and each one teaches me something new about capturing the essence of a moment.

In the end, event photography is about preserving the memories of a shared experience, capturing the energy and joy in a way that makes those moments timeless. It's a reminder of the connections we make, the joy we share, and the moments that define us.

**Creating a Photography Project: A Journey of Discovery**

Starting a photography project is one of the most thrilling ways to enhance your skills, delve into your passions, and stretch the limits of your creativity. It provides a clear focus, a path to follow, and a chance to see the world from a fresh perspective. Unlike individual photos, a project lets you build a narrative, creating a cohesive story that unfolds through your images. Here's my guide to starting your own photography project, step by step, and immersing yourself fully in the experience.

**1. Choose a Theme: Finding Your Story**

Every great photography project begins with a theme that resonates with you. It's the foundation, the "why" behind the project, and it should be something that sparks your curiosity and passion. Ask yourself: what do you love capturing? What stories are you drawn to? Maybe it's nature, with all its seasons and cycles, or perhaps it's the rhythm of city life, full of people and moments that reflect the essence of a place.

Choosing a theme gives your project a purpose. If you're passionate about people, a theme like "Faces of My Neighborhood" can become a powerful collection of candid portraits, each revealing a slice of your community's soul. Or if nature calls to you, a theme like "Wild Blooms" could lead you to capture the beauty of flowers as they shift and evolve throughout the year. This process of choosing a theme is about discovering what excites you and finding a way to communicate that excitement visually. Think of it as picking a story you want to tell, one that's uniquely yours and that only you can capture.

**2. Set Goals: Creating a Vision and a Path Forward**

With your theme chosen, it's time to set some clear, achievable goals. Goals give your project structure and direction, and they help keep you motivated when the initial excitement fades. Start by asking yourself a few key questions: How many photos do I want to take? What's my timeline? Do I want to complete this project within a month, or maybe over the course of a year?

Let's say you decide to capture one photo each week for three months. This regular practice encourages you to stay committed, and with each click, you'll notice yourself improving, both technically and creatively. Your goals should feel inspiring, not overwhelming. They're there to guide you, not to pressure you, so set them in a way that aligns with your lifestyle and your creative flow.

Sometimes, I like to break my goals down further, such as focusing on specific aspects of my theme each week. If I'm photographing urban life, for example, one week might be all about capturing people, while the next could focus on architecture. This approach keeps the project fresh and challenges me to explore different facets of my theme.

**3. Plan Your Shots: Visualizing Your Story**

Once you have a theme and goals, planning your shots is where the excitement starts to build. Imagine the types of scenes, subjects, or details you want to capture. If your theme is "City Life," envision what that looks like to you—is it the bustling crowds, quiet alleyways, or maybe the architecture that defines the skyline? If your theme is more nature-focused, think about the landscapes, textures, or even wildlife that would best convey the story you want to tell.

Create a list of potential locations and ideas. This list doesn't have to be exhaustive; it's more of a guide to keep you inspired and focused. Visit neighborhoods at different times of day to see how the light changes the scene. Or if you're working on a nature project, plan visits to parks or gardens during various seasons to capture the beauty as it shifts and changes.

Planning also helps you anticipate the tools and techniques you might need, whether it's bringing along a certain lens, considering the lighting, or thinking about composition. For me, planning is like sketching out the first draft of a story. It provides a foundation while leaving room for spontaneity, so that when the unexpected happens, you're ready to capture it as part of your narrative.

**4. Experiment and Push Boundaries**

A photography project is the perfect opportunity to step outside your comfort zone and experiment with new techniques. Let yourself play with settings, angles, and perspectives you may not usually consider. If your project is about street photography, try blending into the background and capturing people candidly without them noticing. Or, if it's a landscape project, experiment with different focal lengths or shoot at unusual times of day to create unique effects.

Don't be afraid to make mistakes or take risks. Some of the most creative shots come from happy accidents or moments when you push beyond what feels safe and familiar. Let the project be a space for growth and discovery. By experimenting, you'll not only improve your technical skills but also learn more about your own creative instincts and style.

**5. Review and Reflect on Your Progress**

As you start to accumulate photos, take time to review your work periodically. Look for patterns, styles, or techniques that seem to emerge naturally. Reflect on what resonates with you, what feels true to your theme, and where you might want to improve. This is a moment to evaluate your progress and reconnect with the purpose of your project.

Reviewing your photos also allows you to make adjustments and refine your approach. Maybe you'll notice that certain images evoke a stronger connection to your theme than others. Use this insight to guide the direction of the project as you move forward. Remember, a project is a journey, and part of the beauty is seeing how your vision evolves over time.

### 6. Share Your Work: Telling Your Story to the World

When you feel your project is complete, think about how you'd like to share your work. There are so many possibilities—you could create a photo book, share a series on social media, or even organize a small exhibit. Sharing your work not only celebrates your growth and effort but also allows others to experience the story you've crafted through your images.

Consider writing captions or a brief description for each photo, explaining its place within the project and what it means to you. This adds depth and context, inviting viewers into your perspective and helping them connect more deeply with your work.

### 7. Reflect on the Journey: What Have You Learned?

After completing your project, take some time to reflect on the journey. Think about what you've learned, both about photography and yourself. Did you discover a new aspect of your creative style? Did this project challenge you in unexpected ways? Recognizing the growth you've experienced is a powerful way to appreciate your effort and dedication.

Completing a photography project isn't just about the images—it's about the journey, the lessons, and the stories you've gathered along the way. Each project you undertake brings you closer to your unique voice as a photographer, and each step of the process enriches your understanding of what it means to capture the world through your lens.

### 1. Cameras: Finding the Right Tool for Your Vision

Choosing the right camera can feel like a big decision because it truly shapes how you capture the world. When I first started with photography, I had no idea how much a camera could impact not only the quality of my images but also the way I connect with my subjects and the scene in front of me. Cameras are more than just tools—they're the means through which you express your vision. Let's explore the different types of cameras and how each one brings its own strengths to the table.

**DSLR and Mirrorless Cameras: Powerhouses for Serious Photographers**

If you're passionate about photography, investing in a DSLR or a mirrorless camera can open up new worlds of creativity. These cameras offer interchangeable lenses, manual settings, and often have superior sensors, which means you get more control over the technical aspects of your shots. They're like the painter's palette, giving you full command to create exactly the image you envision.

- **DSLR Cameras: A Traditional Approach with a Hands-On Feel**

My journey with serious photography started with a Canon DSLR, similar to the Canon EOS Rebel T7, and it remains close to my heart as a pivotal step in my learning. DSLRs are known for their optical viewfinders, and there's something incredibly satisfying about seeing the scene through a lens and mirror system that feels tangible. The slight bulkiness of a DSLR can make you feel grounded, connected to the moment you're capturing. I remember peering through that viewfinder and feeling almost like a part of the scene, as if the camera itself were an extension of my eye.

DSLRs are fantastic for those who love that "traditional" photography feel. Looking through an optical viewfinder means you're seeing the world in real-time, untouched by the camera's sensor. It's a pure, direct experience, and for me, that made each shot feel authentic, almost like capturing a memory exactly as I saw it. For anyone who loves feeling in tune with their equipment, DSLRs are an incredible choice.

- **Mirrorless Cameras: Modern, Compact, and Ready for Action**

As I continued exploring photography, I discovered mirrorless cameras, which bring a different experience altogether. Models like the Sony Alpha series opened my eyes to the advantages of a lighter, more compact setup. With a mirrorless camera, the image in the electronic viewfinder shows exactly what the sensor will capture, making it an incredibly precise tool. This real-time feedback lets me adjust exposure, white balance, and other settings with accuracy I couldn't achieve on a DSLR.

Mirrorless cameras are wonderfully intuitive, and they have helped me capture moments in a way that feels immediate and responsive. For example, when I'm photographing fast-moving subjects or working in tricky lighting, seeing exactly how the final shot will look helps me make quick adjustments on the fly. The compact nature of mirrorless systems also means I can carry my camera anywhere without feeling weighed down—a big plus for street and travel photography.

Each of these camera types has its own charm, and choosing between them depends on what feels right for you. The DSLR might appeal if you want a classic, tactile experience, while the mirrorless system is a dream for those who crave flexibility, real-time adjustments, and a lightweight setup. Both are incredibly powerful tools that open up countless creative possibilities.

**Smartphone Cameras: Capturing the World in Your Pocket**

Don't underestimate the power of a good smartphone camera! My iPhone has been a trusty companion for capturing beautiful images on the go, and it continues to amaze me with the quality it can deliver. Modern smartphones like the latest iPhones or Google Pixel phones come equipped with impressive sensors, multiple lenses, and advanced software that make them far more than just convenient—they're genuinely powerful cameras.

With a smartphone, I find myself focusing more on composition and creativity without worrying about settings as much. There's a certain freedom in that simplicity. Smartphones allow you to capture spontaneous moments that would be lost if you had to reach for a larger camera. When I see something interesting or beautiful, all I have to do is pull out my phone and snap the shot—it's instant, intuitive, and surprisingly satisfying.

Smartphones also have the added benefit of being highly portable and discreet, which is perfect for candid or street photography. I love that I can blend into the background more easily and capture life as it happens. Despite their size, today's smartphones can produce stunning results, making them an ideal choice for beginners or anyone who wants to focus on capturing moments without the technicality of a larger camera.

**Choosing What's Right for You**

Each of these camera types has its unique strengths, and they all contribute differently to the way we approach photography. For someone starting out, a smartphone is a fantastic, low-barrier entry into the world of photography. It allows you to explore composition, light, and timing without getting too caught up in settings. As you grow and want more control, stepping into the world of DSLRs or mirrorless cameras can deepen your experience and expand your creative range.

For me, each camera brings out a different aspect of my creativity. My smartphone captures the everyday moments that might otherwise pass by unnoticed. My DSLR connects me to the art of photography in a hands-on, classic way, while my mirrorless camera is my choice for precision and agility. No matter what you choose, remember that the camera is just a tool—the magic comes from how you see the world and the stories you want to tell.

**2. Lenses: Unleashing the Full Potential of Your Camera**

Lenses are where the magic really happens in photography. While the camera captures the shot, the lens shapes it, bringing your vision to life with detail, depth, and character. The lens you choose has a dramatic influence on the quality, feel, and story of your photo. For me, lenses are like different voices, each adding its own nuance to the images I capture. Here's a closer look at some of the lenses I love and why each one has earned its place in my kit.

**Standard Lens (50mm): The All-Rounder**

The 50mm lens—sometimes called the "nifty fifty"—is one of my all-time favorites. It's incredibly versatile, affordable, and sharp, making it a go-to for everything from portraits to street photography. I often use the Canon 50mm f/1.8, and it never fails to capture scenes with a natural look that closely matches how we see the world with our own eyes.

With its wide aperture, the 50mm is perfect for creating that beautiful background blur, or "bokeh," that makes subjects stand out in a soft, dreamy way. This lens has a simplicity to it; it doesn't distort like a wide-angle lens or compress like a telephoto. Instead, it keeps things honest, presenting scenes with clarity and intimacy. It's ideal for capturing authentic, everyday moments, and I find myself reaching for it when I want to emphasize the true essence of my subject without too much distraction.

Whether I'm photographing a friend's portrait or a candid moment on the street, the 50mm allows me to be present with my subject. It's light, compact, and easy to carry around, so it's a natural companion for those days when I just want to get out there and shoot without much fuss.

**Wide-Angle Lens: Expansive Views and Epic Scenery**

If you love landscapes, architecture, or even just dramatic compositions, a wide-angle lens is a must-have. I use the Canon EF-S 10-18mm f/4.5-5.6, and it's been a fantastic tool for capturing expansive scenes that make viewers feel like they're stepping right into the moment.

A wide-angle lens provides an impressive field of view, which is perfect for conveying the vastness and scale of a scene. When I'm out photographing landscapes, I love how this lens captures every detail in a sweeping vista—from the mountains in the distance to the rocks in the foreground. It's also amazing for architecture, allowing me to emphasize the intricate details of buildings while fitting the entire structure into the frame.

Using a wide-angle lens has taught me to think more about composition, as it tends to exaggerate distances and create depth. It challenges me to find leading lines or interesting foreground elements to guide the viewer's eye through the image. I often feel like a wide-angle lens pulls me into a scene, inviting me to explore every part of it—and I hope that's what viewers feel too when they see my photos.

**Telephoto Lens: Bringing Distant Subjects Up Close**

For those times when you can't get physically close to your subject, a telephoto lens is essential. I use the Sony 70-300mm f/4.5-5.6, and it's been an invaluable tool for wildlife and sports photography, as well as any scenario where I want to capture fine details from afar without disturbing the scene.

With a telephoto lens, I can zoom in on distant subjects, whether it's a bird perched high in a tree or an athlete mid-action on the field. There's something thrilling about capturing those moments without intruding, preserving the scene exactly as it is. The compression effect of a telephoto lens also creates a beautiful sense of depth, pulling the background closer and making the subject stand out.

A telephoto lens allows me to stay in the background and observe, almost like a silent witness. It's especially useful in situations where I want to capture genuine expressions or behaviors without being noticed. This lens has taught me the value of patience and observation, reminding me that sometimes, the best photos come from standing back and letting the scene unfold naturally.

**Macro Lens: Exploring a World of Tiny Wonders**

Macro photography is like diving into a hidden world, one filled with tiny, intricate details that often go unnoticed. The Canon 100mm f/2.8 macro lens has opened up an entirely new realm for me, allowing me to capture the fine textures and patterns on flowers, insects, and other small subjects in stunning clarity.

A macro lens lets you get incredibly close to your subject, revealing details that would be impossible to see with the naked eye. I find myself in awe when I capture the delicate veins of a leaf or the minute details on an insect's wing. With macro photography, even the most ordinary subjects become extraordinary, transforming into scenes of unexpected beauty.

This lens has taught me patience and precision, as even the slightest movement can throw off focus. Using a tripod is essential, especially when I'm working with such fine details. I love the focus and calm that macro photography requires; it's almost meditative, encouraging me to slow down and appreciate the beauty in the small things.

**Zoom Lenses: Versatility and Convenience in One Lens**

Zoom lenses are all about versatility, and they're a perfect option for those who want the flexibility to capture a variety of scenes without switching lenses. The Canon EF-S 18-135mm f/3.5-5.6 has become a favorite of mine for travel and everyday photography because it covers a wide range of focal lengths, allowing me to switch from capturing wide scenes to focusing in on details with just one lens.

A zoom lens is like a Swiss Army knife for photographers. Whether I'm photographing a wide landscape, an intimate portrait, or a close-up of a distant building, the zoom lens adapts to whatever I need. It's perfect for those days when I'm not sure what I'll encounter or when I want to keep my kit light and easy to carry.

With a zoom lens, I have the freedom to experiment and adapt to the scene in front of me. It's a great tool for anyone who values convenience and wants the ability to capture a wide variety of images without carrying multiple lenses. This lens has taught me the value of flexibility in photography, reminding me to stay open to the unexpected and to make the most of every opportunity.

**Choosing the Right Lens for Your Vision**

Each lens brings its own personality to a photograph, shaping the way we see and capture the world. Choosing the right lens is about understanding your style and the stories you want to tell. For me, lenses are like different languages, each one helping me express a unique perspective.

Whether it's the simplicity of a 50mm, the grandeur of a wide-angle, the precision of a macro, the intimacy of a telephoto, or the adaptability of a zoom lens, each one plays a crucial role in how I capture and share my view of the world. No matter which lenses you choose, remember that the true magic lies in how you use them to bring your creative vision to life.

**3. Tripods: The Steady Foundation for Every Shot**

A good tripod is like the backbone of photography, especially when you're working with low light, long exposures, or situations where absolute stability is essential. When I first started, I didn't quite understand the importance of a tripod. I thought I could hold the camera steady enough on my own. But as I dove deeper into photography, I realized how crucial a sturdy tripod could be, not only for sharpness but also for creativity.

Brands like Manfrotto and Joby have become my trusted companions for lightweight and stable tripods. These brands offer a range of options that make it easy to find the right fit for different needs. Manfrotto's tripods are robust and perfect for heavier setups, while Joby's flexible, lightweight tripods are ideal for travel or for those moments when I want to set up in unusual places, like wrapping the legs around a tree branch or a railing.

One of my favorite uses for a tripod is for long-exposure photography, where the camera's shutter stays open to capture more light over a longer period. This technique allows me to capture mesmerizing scenes like the smooth flow of a river, the trails of car headlights, or the stars moving across the night sky. Without a tripod, these kinds of shots would be nearly impossible to achieve.

A tripod also gives me the freedom to focus on composition and timing without worrying about stability. When setting up for a cityscape at night or a time-lapse of a sunset, I can adjust my camera precisely, knowing it will stay in place for as long as I need. This reliability opens up a whole world of possibilities, allowing me to experiment with different angles, heights, and perspectives that wouldn't be feasible without a stable base.

A tripod, to me, is more than just a piece of equipment; it's a reliable partner that supports my creative vision. It allows me to slow down, be intentional with my shots, and capture scenes exactly as I imagine them, free from the worries of camera shake or instability.

**4. Lighting Equipment: Crafting the Perfect Light**

Lighting can make or break a photograph. Natural light is beautiful, but it's not always available or controllable, and that's where having the right lighting equipment can elevate your work to a new level. Mastering artificial light has taught me how to take control of a scene and create the mood I want, regardless of the time of day or location. Here are some essential lighting tools that have become invaluable in my kit:

## • External Flash: Power and Precision in Low Light

An external flash is my go-to when natural light just isn't cutting it. While the built-in flash on a camera can work in a pinch, an external flash from brands like Godox offers a whole new level of control. One of the biggest advantages of an external flash is its flexibility—it can be angled, bounced, or diffused, allowing for softer and more natural-looking light. This prevents that harsh, washed-out effect that a built-in flash often produces.

When I'm shooting portraits indoors or capturing moments at events, an external flash lets me illuminate my subject without overwhelming them. I love experimenting with bouncing the light off walls or ceilings to create a softer, more flattering glow. This technique helps to bring out details and adds depth, giving my photos a polished, professional look even in challenging lighting conditions.

## • Reflectors: Shaping and Softening Light

Reflectors are one of the simplest yet most versatile tools in my lighting kit. They're lightweight, easy to carry, and can make a big difference in how light falls on your subject. I often use reflectors from brands like Neewer, which offer a range of options with silver, gold, white, and black surfaces. Each color serves a different purpose, from adding warmth to creating contrast, allowing me to shape the light exactly as I want.

When I'm shooting outdoors, a reflector can help fill in shadows and soften harsh sunlight, creating a balanced and even look. I find reflectors especially useful for portrait photography, where the light needs to be gentle and flattering. With a reflector, I can direct light onto my subject's face, highlighting their features in a natural and beautiful way. It's a simple yet powerful tool that reminds me of the artistry in photography—how small adjustments to light can transform the entire mood of an image.

**• Softboxes and Studio Lights: Crafting Light in Indoor Settings**

For indoor or studio work, softboxes and studio lights are essential tools that allow me to have complete control over lighting. Softboxes, particularly those from brands like Godox and Neewer, create a diffused, even light that's incredibly flattering for portraits. The soft, shadow-free light makes it ideal for capturing details without harsh contrasts, which is especially helpful for product photography or headshots.

Setting up studio lights allows me to experiment with different lighting setups, from high-key bright scenes to low-key dramatic looks. This control over light is what makes studio work so satisfying for me—it's almost like painting with light, where every angle and every intensity brings a new emotion to the image. With a well-placed softbox, I can create the illusion of daylight streaming through a window, or I can sculpt shadows that add depth and mystery.

Lighting equipment has expanded my understanding of photography, teaching me that light is not just an element in a photo but a character with its own role in the story. By mastering these tools, I can create scenes that reflect my vision, regardless of the environment or the time of day.

**5. Accessories: The Small Essentials that Make a Big Difference**
While the camera and lenses are the stars of any photography setup, the right accessories can enhance the entire experience, making each shoot smoother, more organized, and ultimately more enjoyable. I've come to realize that having a few key accessories not only improves my workflow but also protects and enhances my gear. Here are some of my go-to accessories that have become indispensable in my photography kit:

**Memory Cards: Keeping Up with the Pace**

In the world of digital photography, memory cards are essential. I always keep extra memory cards on hand—there's nothing worse than running out of storage in the middle of a shoot! Brands like SanDisk and Lexar are my favorites because of their fast write speeds, which handle high-resolution images and rapid bursts effortlessly.

Having backups ensures I'm never limited by storage, even during longer shoots or when I'm photographing in RAW format, which takes up more space but offers the best image quality. Memory cards may seem like a small detail, but they're the unsung heroes of a shoot. A reliable memory card means I can focus on capturing the moment without worrying about whether my storage will hold up.

**Camera Bag: Keeping Gear Safe and Accessible**

A good camera bag is more than just a bag—it's a mobile workstation. My Canon bag has become a constant companion, protecting my gear and keeping everything organized. A well-organized bag makes it easy to switch lenses, grab memory cards, or reach for a spare battery without having to rummage around.

When I'm out on an all-day shoot, especially in urban settings or while traveling, having a camera bag that's comfortable and secure is a game-changer. The compartments in my bag allow me to keep each piece of gear in its place, reducing the risk of damage and making it easy to find what I need in the moment. Whether I'm working in a crowded city or hiking up a mountain, a reliable bag gives me peace of mind, knowing my equipment is safe, organized, and ready for any situation.

**Lens Filters: Enhancing Creativity and Protecting Lenses**

Lens filters are like adding another layer of versatility to my camera setup. They serve both creative and practical purposes, allowing me to control reflections, contrast, and color while also protecting my lenses. A polarizing filter, for example, is a favorite of mine for outdoor shoots. It reduces glare from reflective surfaces, like water or glass, and enhances the saturation of colors, making skies bluer and foliage richer. This small addition can make landscapes come to life in a way that feels more vibrant and true to the eye.

Another essential filter is the UV filter, which protects the front element of my lenses from dust, scratches, and even minor impacts. It's a simple and affordable way to protect an investment in expensive glass, adding peace of mind whenever I'm shooting in challenging environments. Lens filters remind me that even small accessories can significantly enhance the quality and safety of my equipment, allowing me to push creative boundaries without sacrificing the integrity of my gear.

**Cleaning Kit: Keeping Everything Crystal Clear**

Photography is all about clarity, so keeping lenses and sensors clean is crucial. A cleaning kit with microfiber cloths and brushes from brands like Giottos has been invaluable in maintaining my gear. I remember a time when a tiny speck of dust on my lens ruined an otherwise perfect shot, and since then, I've made regular cleaning a habit.

Dust spots and smudges can be distracting, especially in high-resolution images, where every detail is magnified. By regularly cleaning my lenses and sensor, I ensure that my images are as sharp and clear as possible. My cleaning kit includes tools like an air blower to gently remove dust and soft microfiber cloths that keep my lenses scratch-free. Having these tools on hand means I can quickly address any dust or smudges, even in the middle of a shoot, ensuring that each shot remains pristine.

**Why Accessories Matter**

These accessories may seem like small additions, but they play a vital role in my photography routine. Memory cards keep me prepared, a good bag keeps me organized, filters add creative control, and a cleaning kit keeps everything sharp and clear. Together, they allow me to focus on what truly matters: capturing the beauty of the world around me.

Each of these accessories has become more than just a tool; they're part of my process, ensuring that I'm ready for any moment and that my gear stays in top condition. They allow me to work with confidence, knowing that I have everything I need to handle whatever the day—or my creative vision—throws my way.

Let me know if this expanded version captures the depth and personal touch you're looking for or if there's anything specific you'd like me to refine!

**Conclusion: Embracing the Journey of Photography**

Investing in the right equipment and accessories is a commitment to your growth as a photographer. Each tool you add to your collection becomes a part of your journey, shaping the way you capture and interpret the world around you. Start with what fits your budget and feels right for where you are in your journey. With time, as your skills evolve and your style emerges, don't hesitate to upgrade or expand your toolkit. But remember, it's not about having the latest gear or the most expensive lenses; it's about using the equipment you have to tell stories that are uniquely yours, to capture moments that resonate with who you are.

Looking back on my own path, I remember the thrill of upgrading my first lens, the excitement that came with adding a new piece of equipment, and how each new tool opened up fresh possibilities. But along the way, I realized that while gear can help you achieve certain effects, the true power of a photograph lies in the eye and heart behind the camera. Some of the most meaningful images I've taken weren't because of top-of-the-line equipment—they were simply moments that spoke to me, captured with whatever I had in my hands at that time.

As you grow, take the time to explore and understand what equipment truly resonates with you. Don't feel pressured to follow trends or to chase after the newest releases. Let your choices reflect your personal style and the unique perspective you bring to the world. Photography is a journey, and building your kit is part of that journey. Each investment, whether it's a high-quality lens or a simple accessory, is a step toward refining your craft, shaping your style, and discovering your own voice as an artist.

Enjoy every moment of learning and experimenting. Every click of the shutter, every piece of equipment added, every new technique mastered—it all becomes part of the story you're creating, both in your work and in your life as a photographer. The camera becomes more than just a tool; it becomes a trusted companion, guiding you through quiet moments and thrilling adventures alike, capturing not only images but memories and experiences that will stay with you.

So embrace each step, each success, and each mistake, knowing that photography isn't about chasing perfection. It's about capturing what moves you, what speaks to your heart, and what you believe is worth sharing with others. It's a journey of exploration and expression, one where you'll continually grow, change, and rediscover the world around you through fresh eyes.

In the end, remember that the essence of photography isn't in perfect settings or flawless gear—it's in those genuine, heartfelt moments that make life beautiful. So keep your curiosity alive, trust your instincts, and let each photo you take bring you closer to understanding not only the world around you but also yourself. And as you go, may your journey be as fulfilling as the images you capture, one frame at a time.

## Practical Tips for Photography Assignments: Embracing Every Opportunity

Embarking on a photography assignment is always an exciting journey, filled with anticipation, curiosity, and maybe a hint of nervous energy. I vividly remember my first assignments—how each one brought a mix of thrill and the unknown, where every new shoot felt like an adventure into uncharted territory. Over time, I've gathered a collection of practical tips that have been invaluable in helping me navigate the diverse demands of photography assignments, whether I'm capturing the intimacy of a wedding, the energy of an event, or the subtle nuances in a portrait. Here are some of my go-to strategies that help me feel prepared and inspired every time I step behind the camera.

### 1. Pre-Planning: Setting the Foundation for Success

Pre-planning might seem like a straightforward step, but I've found it to be the backbone of every successful shoot. Proper preparation not only sets the tone for the assignment but also allows me to connect with clients and better understand their vision. For me, this stage is about more than just logistics—it's about building trust and laying the groundwork for a smooth and enjoyable experience for everyone involved.

- **Understand the Brief: Getting to the Heart of the Client's Vision**

Before I dive into any assignment, I make it a priority to have a thorough discussion with my client. These conversations go beyond a list of must-have shots; they're a chance for me to truly understand the client's vision and preferences. I ask questions about the mood they want, the style they envision, and if there are specific shots or moments they're especially excited about. I've come to love this process because it gives me insight into what's important to them. Knowing these details not only guides my approach but also helps me capture images that hold meaning for them—whether it's a particular lighting style, a cherished location, or a candid moment they want preserved.

## • Scout the Location: Discovering the Scene Before the Action Begins

If I have the opportunity, I always make time to visit the location before the day of the shoot. Exploring the space in advance allows me to assess the environment, observe how light interacts with the area, and think about potential compositions. During my location scout, I'll often look for hidden gems—unexpected backgrounds, natural lighting pockets, or architectural elements that might add character to the photos.

Scouting also helps me feel more confident when the day of the assignment arrives. I know the layout, I've considered the lighting at different times of day, and I have a mental map of where to set up for specific shots. Sometimes, this pre-visit also sparks creative ideas I wouldn't have thought of otherwise, like framing shots around unique details or using reflections to add depth. It's these small details that can make a significant difference in the final result, and having a mental plan in place keeps me focused and relaxed, ready to adapt to whatever comes my way.

**Create a Shot List: Capturing Every Important Moment with Intention**

Having a shot list has become one of my most valuable tools—a sort of secret weapon that ensures I capture every essential moment without missing a beat. Early in my career, I learned that even with the best intentions, it's easy to get swept up in the flow of a shoot and accidentally overlook key shots. Now, creating a shot list is a ritual that helps me stay grounded and focused, giving me the confidence to approach each assignment with clarity and purpose.

For me, the process of building a shot list starts by envisioning the entire assignment from beginning to end. I think about the must-have shots, like the pivotal moments and key scenes that the client will want to remember. If it's a wedding, that list might include everything from the first look and the exchange of vows to candid moments of laughter during the reception. If it's an event, I'll make sure to capture the energy and emotion in both big moments and the quieter, more intimate interactions. The shot list becomes a roadmap for the day, allowing me to move through the event with a clear sense of purpose.

I've also found that sharing this shot list with my clients beforehand is a powerful way to collaborate and make sure I'm aligned with their vision. It opens up a conversation where they can add their input, suggesting additional shots that might hold special meaning for them. This collaborative approach not only makes the client feel more involved but also enriches the final collection, ensuring it's filled with moments that are deeply personal and meaningful.

Beyond capturing the essentials, a shot list also frees up mental space, allowing me to get creative once I've covered the basics. Knowing that I've captured all the "must-haves" gives me the freedom to experiment with angles, lighting, or spontaneous compositions. I can relax into the flow of the shoot, trusting that I'm prepared and that nothing important will slip through the cracks. It's a way to stay organized and reduce stress, making the experience enjoyable for both me and the client.

Ultimately, the shot list is more than just a checklist; it's a tool that helps me deliver a collection of images that tells a complete story. It's about honoring the client's vision while also allowing space for creativity and spontaneity. Each time I use it, I'm reminded that even the simplest of tools can make a significant difference in creating a final product that resonates, capturing the essence of the moment with care and attention.

**Gear Preparation: Ensuring Every Detail is Ready for Success**

Gear preparation has become a crucial part of my photography routine—one of those essential rituals that I never skip. It may sound simple, but taking the time to meticulously check and prepare my equipment has saved me from countless potential mishaps. Knowing my gear is ready allows me to focus fully on the creative aspects of the shoot, without distractions or worries about technical issues. Here's how I approach gear preparation to ensure that every shoot goes smoothly and that I'm free to capture the best moments as they unfold.

### • Check Your Equipment: The Power of a Simple Habit

I can't emphasize enough how important it is to check all of your equipment before a shoot. It's one of those habits that may seem minor, but it has a huge impact on the flow of the day. Before each assignment, I go through every piece of gear, making sure my camera body, lenses, and accessories are in perfect condition. This includes inspecting my lenses for dust or smudges, adjusting any settings that might need fine-tuning, and ensuring my tripod or stabilizer is ready to go.

Charging batteries and formatting memory cards are at the top of my checklist. There's nothing worse than realizing mid-shoot that your battery is running low or that your memory card is almost full. By charging everything to 100% and clearing my cards, I eliminate any interruptions that could pull me out of the moment. This simple habit gives me peace of mind, allowing me to focus on capturing the energy and emotion of the event without any technical distractions.

### • Bring Backup Gear: Preparing for the Unexpected

If there's one thing I've learned, it's that unexpected situations can and will happen. To prepare for the unpredictable, I always pack backup equipment. My backup kit includes an extra camera body, a versatile lens, additional memory cards, and sometimes even a spare battery charger. Having these backups isn't just a precaution; it's a confidence booster. Knowing that I have a plan B allows me to shoot freely and take creative risks without the constant worry of potential malfunctions.

This approach came in handy on a recent shoot when my main camera unexpectedly froze up. Thankfully, I had my backup camera ready to go, and within minutes, I was back in action without missing a beat. It's these moments that remind me why I put in the extra effort to prepare—having a backup ensures that no precious moments are lost and that I can keep my focus on the unfolding story.

Gear preparation may seem like a small part of the process, but it's the foundation that supports everything else. By ensuring my equipment is ready, I'm setting myself up for success and creating a stress-free environment where creativity can thrive. It's a simple yet powerful habit that I carry into every shoot, reminding me that even the smallest details can make a world of difference.

**Different Types of Photography Assignments: Exploring Your Craft One Project at a Time**

Diving into different photography assignments is like embarking on a series of mini-adventures, each one offering new challenges, insights, and opportunities to grow as a photographer. I've found that experimenting with varied assignments not only hones my technical skills but also opens up different perspectives on how to capture and tell stories through my lens. Here's a closer look at some types of assignments I recommend, each with its own unique focus and goals.

**1. Portrait Photography Assignment: Capturing Personality Through Light**

- **Task:** Capture three friends or family members in different lighting conditions—natural, artificial, and a mix of both.

- **Goal:** Portrait photography is all about capturing the essence of a person, and this assignment is a beautiful opportunity to experiment with how light can change a mood or highlight unique features. Try positioning your subjects in different locations, using window light for a soft, natural look, or try artificial lighting to create a more dramatic effect. I've learned that small shifts in shadow, highlights, and contrast can reveal different sides of a person's character, whether it's their confidence, playfulness, or introspection. Play with different poses and expressions to create portraits that genuinely reflect each individual's personality.

**2. Street Photography Challenge: The Art of Spontaneous Storytelling**

- **Task:** Spend an afternoon wandering through your local city, capturing candid moments of everyday life.

- **Goal:** Street photography has a special place in my heart because it's a raw, honest way to capture life as it happens. It's about storytelling, observing without interfering, and finding beauty in the unexpected. Every street corner, every market, every park can hold a story waiting to be told. Let yourself blend into the environment, allowing those unplanned moments—like a smile exchanged between strangers or the quiet focus of someone reading on a bench—to unfold. This assignment will sharpen your sense of timing and teach you to see the world with fresh eyes, always ready to capture the essence of a place and its people.

### 3. Wedding Photography Experience: Capturing Emotion Amidst Chaos

- **Task:** Offer to assist a professional wedding photographer or document a friend's wedding as a second shooter.

- **Goal:** Weddings are a whirlwind of emotions, from the joy and excitement to the quiet, tender moments between loved ones. As a wedding photographer, you're not just documenting an event—you're capturing memories that will be cherished for a lifetime. This assignment teaches you to work quickly, adapt to ever-changing lighting, and prioritize shots to ensure you don't miss those once-in-a-lifetime moments. Working in this fast-paced environment helps you develop strong time-management skills and the ability to capture genuine emotions, turning fleeting moments into beautiful, lasting memories.

### 4. Nature and Landscape Photography: Patience and the Power of Light

- **Task:** Plan a weekend trip to a nearby national park or nature reserve, photographing landscapes at different times of the day—sunrise, midday, and sunset.

- **Goal:** Nature photography has taught me to slow down and really appreciate the beauty of the world around me. This assignment is a chance to experiment with composition, foreground interest, and how natural light shapes a scene. I've discovered that the same landscape can look completely different depending on the time of day. This exercise encourages patience and mindfulness, as you wait for the perfect light to bring out the scene's colors and textures. It's about finding peace in the stillness and learning to see landscapes as more than just scenery—they become stories of nature unfolding in front of you.

## 5. Food Photography Practice: Creating a Feast for the Eyes

- **Task:** Prepare a dish and stage it for a photoshoot at home. Play around with various angles, props, and natural light to showcase your culinary creation.

- **Goal:** Food photography is incredibly satisfying because it combines art, styling, and lighting in a way that makes a simple dish look irresistible. Experiment with textures, colors, and props to create a visually appealing setup. Consider using fresh ingredients, cutlery, or a rustic backdrop to enhance the composition. This assignment not only helps you develop an eye for detail but also teaches you how to control lighting to make the food appear both appetizing and beautiful. Plus, it's a fun way to play with color and composition, adding your own creative flair to something as everyday as a meal.

## 6. Event Photography Assignment: Capturing the Energy of a Moment

- **Task:** Volunteer to photograph a local event, like a festival or community gathering.

- **Goal:** Event photography is all about capturing the energy and spirit of a gathering. This assignment encourages you to stay alert and responsive, always ready for those moments of genuine interaction and excitement. Documenting an event pushes you to manage dynamic lighting, adapt quickly to different settings, and capture candid emotions that tell a complete story. It's a fantastic way to build versatility and connect with your subjects through the lens, preserving the event's unique atmosphere in each shot.

**Exercises for Skill Improvement: Building Habits for Creative Growth**

To improve as a photographer, I've found it valuable to set aside time for skill-building exercises that push me beyond my comfort zone. Here are a few exercises that have helped me grow:

- **Timed Shoot:** Set a timer for 15 minutes and challenge yourself to take as many photos as you can. This exercise encourages quick thinking and forces you to make creative choices on the spot, helping you develop a more intuitive shooting style.

- **Theme Challenge:** Choose a theme for a week (like "shadows" or "reflections") and capture photos that fit this theme each day. By focusing on a theme, you sharpen your eye for detail and begin to notice subjects or compositions that might have gone overlooked.

- **Editing Practice:** After each assignment, select a few photos to edit in different styles—high contrast, vintage, soft, etc. Experimenting with various editing techniques helps you discover what aesthetics resonate with you and how to use editing to enhance storytelling and mood.

**Reflection and Evaluation: Learning from Every Assignment**

After completing each assignment, I always take a moment to reflect and evaluate my work. This reflection allows me to learn from each experience and build on my skills.

- **What aspects of the assignment did you enjoy the most?** Identifying what you enjoy helps guide you toward the types of photography you're most passionate about, shaping future projects and helping you refine your unique style.

- **What challenges did you encounter, and how did you overcome them?** Noting challenges and solutions is a valuable learning tool, helping you remember what worked so you can apply it in future shoots.

• **What will you do differently in future assignments?** Each assignment is a learning experience. Thinking about what you might adjust next time allows you to grow as a photographer, continuously refining your approach.

**Conclusion: Embrace the Journey of Discovery**

Engaging in different types of photography assignments is more than just a way to build skills; it's a path to discovering what you truly love about photography. Each assignment presents its own set of challenges and joys, encouraging you to explore, experiment, and create visuals that tell your unique story. Embrace these challenges, learn from each experience, and enjoy the journey of refining your craft. The more you step outside your comfort zone, the more you'll uncover the endless possibilities of photography.

## 1. The Basics of Composition

When I first picked up a camera, I quickly realized that composition is where the magic happens. It's the art of arranging elements within your frame to create visually stunning and engaging photographs. A well-composed shot can transform an ordinary scene into something truly captivating, inviting the viewer to see the world through your eyes. Here are some foundational techniques I've learned along the way that can help you elevate your photography:

• **Rule of Thirds:**

This technique was a game-changer for me. Imagine dividing your image into a 3x3 grid. By placing important elements along these lines or at their intersections, you create balance and intrigue. It's like giving your viewer a guided tour through your image, drawing them naturally to the focal points. For me, it added structure to my compositions, making my shots feel more intentional and compelling. I've found that even a slight adjustment, like moving the subject just off-center, can turn a simple scene into something that feels more dynamic and balanced.

- **Leading Lines:**

I love using natural lines found in my surroundings—like roads, fences, or rivers—to lead the viewer's gaze toward the main subject. It adds depth and a sense of movement to my photographs. The way a winding path can draw you in is something truly special, guiding the viewer's eye through the scene and creating a journey within the frame. Leading lines create a sense of direction, making the viewer feel like they're part of the story unfolding within the photo.

- **Framing:**

This technique is one of my favorites. By incorporating surrounding elements—like tree branches, windows, or doorways—to frame my subject, I create a sense of isolation that helps the subject pop while providing context. It's like saying, "Look here! This is important!" Framing can also add layers of storytelling by providing hints about the environment or mood, giving the viewer a sense of place and context without overwhelming the main subject. I love experimenting with different natural or architectural frames to create depth and draw the viewer's eye exactly where I want it.

- **Symmetry and Patterns:**

I've found that symmetry creates a feeling of harmony in my images, a sense of visual balance that's deeply satisfying. Whenever I spot a pattern or repeating shape, I can't resist capturing it. Symmetry can be striking, providing a calming effect that appeals to our natural love for order. At the same time, I enjoy exploring asymmetry, which adds dynamic tension and keeps the viewer's eye moving across the composition. Patterns, whether in nature or in urban settings, bring a rhythm to my photos, transforming ordinary scenes into something mesmerizing. I find that breaking a pattern with a unique element can create even more interest.

- **Negative Space:**

Embracing empty space in my compositions has been liberating. Using negative space effectively can emphasize the subject, making it stand out without distractions. It's like giving the viewer room to breathe and appreciate the essence of the subject. Negative space simplifies the scene, bringing a calm focus to the composition and making the subject's impact more powerful. This approach works wonders in minimalist compositions, allowing one subject to dominate the frame and capture attention. I often use negative space to convey a feeling of solitude or contemplation, creating a quiet, reflective atmosphere in my images.

By incorporating these techniques into my photography, I've been able to create images that resonate with my audience and capture the stories I want to tell. Composition is not just about arranging elements; it's about conveying emotion and narrative through each frame. The beauty of photography is that these techniques can be combined and adapted in countless ways, allowing you to discover your own style and unique voice.

## 2. Exploring Photography Styles

Photography is a vast playground filled with different styles, each offering a unique approach and techniques. Understanding these styles has inspired me and helped me discover my artistic preferences. While **styles** focus on how a photo is captured and the techniques involved, **subjects** center on what is captured—such as people, places, or objects. Here, I'll share some photography styles that I've enjoyed exploring, each bringing a unique perspective to my work.

- **Portrait Photography**:

This style has always fascinated me. Capturing the personality and essence of individuals or groups allows me to tell a story through their expressions. I love experimenting with lighting and poses to highlight features and convey emotions. Changing up backgrounds can add depth and make portraits even more impactful. Portrait photography is about creating an intimate connection between the subject and the viewer.

**• Landscape Photography:**

There's something magical about capturing the beauty of nature. I find immense joy in photographing wide-open spaces, mountains, and oceans. It's about understanding light and composition to evoke a sense of place. Each time I set out to photograph a landscape, I feel connected to the environment in a profound way, as if I'm capturing a slice of the natural world's vastness and serenity.

**• Street Photography:**

I thrive on the spontaneity of street photography. It's all about capturing candid moments of everyday life and telling stories through these interactions. I always keep my camera ready to document unique scenes that showcase the human experience in public spaces. It's exhilarating! Street photography is a raw, unscripted glimpse into real life, allowing me to capture the pulse of a place.

**• Macro Photography:**

Delving into the world of macro photography has opened my eyes to details I often overlooked. Capturing extreme close-ups of small subjects—like insects or flowers—has taught me to appreciate the beauty in the little things. It requires patience and precision, but the results are worth it, revealing intricate patterns and textures that might otherwise go unnoticed.

**• Documentary Photography:**

I've been drawn to documentary photography for its storytelling aspect. It's about capturing significant events, social issues, and cultural narratives. I find that this style requires a thoughtful approach, allowing me to evoke emotions and provoke thought through my images. Documentary photography preserves moments of truth and can bring attention to stories that need to be told.

• **Architectural Photography**:

There's a certain beauty in capturing buildings and structures. Understanding perspectives, lines, and light enhances the form and function of architectural designs. It's fascinating to see how architecture interacts with its environment, showcasing the vision behind each design while emphasizing its structural elegance.

Exploring these various styles has enriched my photography journey. Each style offers a different perspective and set of skills, encouraging me to experiment with technique and creativity. I encourage you to try out different styles and even mix elements from them to develop your unique artistic voice. Embrace the process, and let your creativity flow!

## 3. Editing and Post-Processing for Beginners

Once I've captured a photo, the next crucial step is editing and post-processing. This stage is where a good shot can become a truly stunning image. Editing allows me to refine details, correct any issues, and add my personal touch, enhancing the mood and story I want to convey. Editing isn't about completely changing a photo; it's about enhancing what's already there, highlighting the best aspects, and keeping the final image aligned with my vision.

When I first started editing, it was overwhelming to understand all the tools and techniques available. However, with practice, I found a workflow that felt natural and helped me achieve a balanced, polished look without overdoing it. In this chapter, I'll guide you through the basics of editing, share some key tools that have made a difference for me, and discuss how to keep that natural look in your photos while still making an impact.

### Getting Started: Choosing the Right Software

There are several editing programs out there, each offering different features. For beginners, I recommend starting with user-friendly software like **Adobe Lightroom** or **Photoshop**. Lightroom is perfect for global adjustments, such as color correction and exposure changes, while Photoshop offers more in-depth retouching options for those looking to explore more advanced techniques. Both programs are industry standards and provide a solid foundation for anyone serious about editing. If you're looking for free alternatives, **GIMP** and **Canva** also offer great features for basic edits.

**Key Adjustments to Start With**

**1. Exposure and Brightness**:

The first thing I check is the exposure. Sometimes, photos can turn out too dark or too bright, depending on lighting conditions. Adjusting exposure and brightness levels ensures that your subject is visible and that details aren't lost. It's about finding a balance so the photo feels natural but still clear and defined.

**2. Contrast**:

Contrast adds depth to an image by enhancing the difference between light and dark areas. A higher contrast can make a photo more dramatic, while lower contrast softens the look. I love using contrast to create mood; for example, boosting contrast in black-and-white photos can make them look more striking and timeless.

**3. Color Temperature and White Balance**:

White balance corrects the color tones in an image, making it look warmer (more yellow) or cooler (more blue). This setting is crucial in achieving a realistic color tone, especially in outdoor or mixed-light conditions. By adjusting the white balance, you can bring out warmer, softer tones for a cozy feel or cooler tones for a crisp, clean look.

**4. Saturation and Vibrance**:

These tools control the intensity of colors. Saturation boosts all colors equally, which can sometimes look unnatural if overdone. Vibrance, on the other hand, targets only the duller colors, preserving skin tones and preventing the photo from looking too processed. For natural-looking results, I usually prefer to work with vibrance instead of heavy saturation.

## 5. Sharpness and Clarity:

Increasing sharpness brings out fine details, especially in textures. Clarity enhances mid-tones, adding definition to the image without making it appear too harsh. These adjustments can help make your subject stand out, particularly in portrait or landscape photography, where texture and detail add a lot to the photo's character.

**Advanced Edits: Taking It a Step Further**

Once you feel comfortable with the basics, you might want to explore some advanced editing techniques. These techniques allow for more creative freedom and can make your photos truly unique.

- **Dodge and Burn:**

Dodging (lightening) and burning (darkening) specific areas can help shape your image by drawing attention to certain parts. For example, lightening a person's face while darkening the background subtly makes them pop without looking over-edited. This technique is commonly used in portrait photography to add depth and focus.

- **Selective Adjustments:**

Sometimes, you only want to edit a specific part of the photo, like enhancing the color of the sky in a landscape or bringing out the details in someone's eyes. Selective adjustments allow you to apply changes only where needed, giving you more control over the final look.

- **Color Grading:**

Color grading lets you add a unique color tone to your images, often used to create a consistent style or mood across a series of photos.

Whether you're aiming for warm, earthy tones or cool, desaturated looks, color grading can make your photos feel more cohesive and visually striking.

**Keeping a Natural Look**

One of the challenges with editing is maintaining a natural look while still enhancing the image. Over-editing can make photos look artificial, so I try to follow the "less is more" approach. Subtlety is key; sometimes, a small adjustment is all it takes to transform an image without losing its authenticity. For instance, instead of over-sharpening or saturating, I'll focus on refining the colors and tones in a way that complements the photo rather than overpowering it.

**Building Your Workflow**

Having a workflow makes the editing process smoother and more efficient. Here's my typical workflow:

1. **Start with Exposure and White Balance**: Get the basic lighting and color temperature right first. This gives a solid foundation for other adjustments.

2. **Adjust Contrast and Clarity**: Add depth and detail without overdoing it. This step brings out the subject's texture and definition.

3. **Enhance Colors**: Use vibrance or selective color adjustments to make specific tones stand out.

4. **Apply Selective Edits if Needed**: If there are parts of the image that need special attention, like brightening the subject or deepening the sky, this is the stage to focus on them.

5. **Final Touches**: Apply sharpening, reduce noise if needed, and add any minor adjustments to finalize the image.

**Editing Tools I Recommend**

There are many tools out there, but here are a few that have helped me bring my vision to life:

- **Lightroom**: Great for batch editing and organizing your photos, making it easy to apply adjustments across multiple images.

- **Photoshop**: Offers more advanced retouching and manipulation tools, ideal for in-depth editing.

- **Luminar Neo**: Luminar Neo is an intuitive program with AI-powered tools that simplify editing, especially for landscapes and portraits. It offers a range of creative effects and quick adjustments, making it ideal for both beginners and more experienced photographers.

- **Snapseed**: A free mobile app with powerful editing options, including selective adjustments and tools to refine photos.

## Practice Makes Perfect

Editing is a skill that grows with time and practice. The more you experiment with different tools and styles, the more you'll develop your own unique editing style. Don't be afraid to try new techniques or take creative risks; editing is where you can really let your personality shine through.

By mastering the basics and gradually incorporating more advanced techniques, you can create images that stand out and truly reflect your creative vision. Remember, editing is an extension of your photography—it's a way to enhance what you've captured and make it resonate even more deeply with viewers.

## Where to Find Affordable Photography Gear

When you're passionate about photography but don't want to break the bank, finding affordable gear can be a challenge. Fortunately, with the internet, there are plenty of platforms offering good-quality equipment at lower prices, no matter where you are in the world. Whether you're looking for a new lens, camera body, or accessories, these global marketplaces give you the chance to find the perfect gear without overspending. Here's a list of some of the best places to start your search for affordable photography equipment:

### 1. eBay

eBay is one of the largest platforms for buying both new and used products, and photography gear is no exception. You can find everything from cameras and lenses to tripods and other accessories at great prices. With sellers from all over the world, you can compare prices across different countries and score the best deals.

### 2. Amazon

Amazon is another global platform where you can find both new and used photography equipment. They often run promotions or clearance sales, and you can sometimes find refurbished cameras and lenses at a fraction of the original price. Just be sure to check seller ratings and reviews before making a purchase.

### 3. MPB

MPB is a dedicated platform for buying and selling used camera gear. They specialize in photography equipment, and their inventory is constantly updated with cameras, lenses, and accessories from top brands. MPB thoroughly inspects each item, so you know exactly what condition it's in before buying. They ship to many countries worldwide.

### 4. KEH Camera

KEH Camera is another trusted source for used photography gear. Based in the U.S., they ship internationally and have a wide selection of cameras, lenses, and accessories at lower prices than retail. Their gear is graded based on condition, and they offer warranties, so you can shop with confidence.

### 5. B&H Photo Video

B&H is a well-known name in the photography world, and while they primarily sell new gear, they also have a robust used section. Their selection is vast, and they ship globally. Keep an eye out for sales, especially around holidays, when you can find significant discounts on both new and used gear.

### 6. Adorama

Adorama is similar to B&H, offering both new and used camera gear. They also have frequent deals and promotions, particularly on bundles that include cameras and accessories. Like the others, they ship worldwide and provide international customer support

### 7. AliExpress

If you're looking for budget-friendly photography accessories like tripods, filters, or camera bags, AliExpress is worth checking out. While it's wise to be cautious about the quality of some items, there are plenty of highly-rated sellers offering decent products at low prices. They ship globally, though delivery can sometimes take longer.

No matter where you shop, it's always a good idea to read reviews, compare prices, and ensure the seller or platform is reliable before making a purchase. Happy hunting!

**Our Photography Journey**

Photography is so much more than capturing beautiful images—it's a doorway to new experiences, connections, and perspectives. Every time we pick up a camera, we're not only capturing moments but also opening ourselves up to a world of possibilities. It's a journey that lets us see the beauty in the everyday, embrace creativity, and connect with people we might never have met otherwise.

Through photography, we get to meet people from all walks of life, whether it's a quick exchange with a stranger on the street, an in-depth portrait session, or a shared laugh during an event. Each encounter adds depth to our experiences and reminds us of the countless stories that exist all around us. Photography is as much about people and relationships as it is about technique; it invites us to step outside our comfort zones and connect with others in a truly meaningful way.

The joy of photography also lies in its endless possibilities. There's always something new to explore—different styles, techniques, and perspectives that keep our curiosity alive. Whether you're experimenting with street photography, trying out macro shots, or capturing vast landscapes, every photo is an opportunity to express yourself and tell a story.

And perhaps one of the greatest rewards of photography is the chance to rediscover the world through fresh eyes. We start to notice things we might have overlooked before: the way light filters through the trees, the colors in a sunset, or the expressions of people as they go about their day. Photography helps us appreciate the beauty in small moments and reminds us to pause and take it all in.

As you continue on this journey, embrace the adventure of learning, experimenting, and connecting. Photography will take you places you never expected, and each click of the shutter is a chance to capture something extraordinary. So keep exploring, keep meeting new people, and most importantly, keep enjoying every moment that photography brings.

Photography also offers us the incredible gift of lifelong growth. With each photo we take, we learn something new—whether it's about lighting, timing, or even ourselves. Sometimes, a single image can surprise us, showing us a side of our creativity we didn't know we had. And as we continue, we start to build not just a portfolio, but a personal journey told through images. Each photo becomes a part of our story, a reminder of where we've been and how far we've come.

What's even more rewarding is that photography gives us a way to share these discoveries with others. Our images can spark conversations, bring people together, and even inspire others to see the world differently. Sharing our work is like opening a window into our perspective, inviting others to see what we see and feel what we feel. Whether we're displaying our photos in a gallery, sharing them online, or simply showing them to friends, we're connecting with others in a unique and powerful way.

And as we grow and improve, we're reminded that there's no final destination in photography—only new paths to explore. Each photo we take, each moment we capture, is a step forward on an endless journey. Photography keeps us curious, challenging us to keep learning, experimenting, and pushing our creative boundaries. No matter how experienced we become, there's always something new to discover.

So, as you continue on your photography journey, remember to embrace the process, with all its ups and downs. Cherish the connections, the surprises, and the joy of each new discovery. Photography is a world of endless possibilities, and each shot brings you one step closer to capturing something truly meaningful.

Enjoy every moment, every click, and every opportunity to see the world in your own unique way.

**The Future of Photography – What Lies Ahead for Us**

When I look back on my photography journey, it's amazing to see how technology has shaped my path. I started with an iPhone 8+, capturing moments of everyday life without much thought to technique. Today, I'm out on the streets with my Canon, seeking those raw, spontaneous scenes that tell a story. The tools we use have changed so much, yet the essence of photography remains the same. What excites me now is thinking about the future—where photography is heading and how upcoming advancements will open up new ways to express ourselves and connect with others.

## AI and the Changing Game

AI has begun to change the process of capturing and editing photos. I admit, I was a bit hesitant at first. The idea of a program automatically enhancing my photos felt like it might take away from the personal touch I've always tried to maintain in my work. But now, I can see how AI is more of an assistant than a replacement.

For example, software like Lightroom has started to use AI to adjust exposure, highlights, and shadows, and it's surprisingly good. It doesn't always get it right, but it saves me time. I imagine in the near future, AI will get even better at understanding the style each photographer prefers. Maybe one day, it will even be able to edit a photo with the same nuance and subtlety I would—though I'm not quite sure how I feel about that yet. There's something special about the hands-on work of fine-tuning an image that I wouldn't want to lose.

At the same time, I can't deny the potential AI has to open new creative possibilities. Imagine being able to visualize an idea, and within seconds, have an AI create a rough sketch based on your description. It could be a valuable tool for pre-visualizing scenes, experimenting with lighting setups, or even creating unique compositions that inspire further exploration with a real camera. The key, I believe, will be finding the right balance—using AI as a tool to enhance our creativity without letting it take over the art itself.

### The Evolution of Camera Technology

Then there's the advancement in camera technology itself. We've already seen huge leaps with mirrorless systems, faster autofocus, and higher megapixels.

But it's hard not to wonder—what's next? Cameras are becoming smarter, with built-in AI features that recognize faces, animals, and even specific scenes. It's incredible how a camera can now identify the subject and make real-time adjustments, almost as if it's developing its own sense of awareness. The future might hold even smarter cameras that are more intuitive and adaptive, adjusting seamlessly to our style and preferences.

Another exciting possibility is how compact and powerful cameras are becoming. Imagine a world where the quality of a DSLR fits in the palm of your hand, allowing photographers to move freely without the weight of traditional gear. I can see how this would especially benefit street and travel photographers, capturing high-quality images with a device that doesn't draw attention. With this evolution, I think photography will become even more accessible to everyone, regardless of budget or experience level.

### Virtual Reality and Augmented Reality

I can't help but think about how virtual reality (VR) and augmented reality (AR) could change the way we experience photography. Imagine putting on a VR headset and stepping into a 360-degree image, feeling as if you're actually standing in the scene. This could transform the way we share and view travel photography, for instance. Instead of a simple picture, viewers could immerse themselves in a landscape, hearing the sounds and feeling the ambiance as if they were really there.

AR also holds promise for photographers, offering the potential to overlay information in real-time while shooting. Imagine having a tool that not only shows your composition grid but also suggests framing adjustments or lighting tweaks based on the environment around you. These technologies could serve as real-time guides, helping photographers capture the perfect shot while still allowing room for creative intuition.

### Social Media and the Changing Landscape of Photography

Social media has already reshaped photography, making it more accessible but also more competitive. I imagine this trend will continue, with new platforms and ways to share work emerging. Photography might become even more interactive, with tools allowing viewers to engage with photos in new ways, like adjusting the angle or zooming in to explore details. It's a double-edged sword; on one hand, we have more opportunities than ever to showcase our work, but on the other, it can sometimes feel overwhelming to keep up.

As the landscape changes, I think the emphasis will shift toward authenticity. People are starting to crave genuine, unfiltered content that feels personal and real. This could push photographers to focus less on perfection and more on storytelling, capturing moments that truly resonate rather than chasing likes or algorithms. There's a certain beauty in this shift, as it encourages photographers to reconnect with the original purpose of the art form: to capture meaningful moments.

**The Human Element – What Can't Be Replaced**

Despite all the advancements, I believe there's something timeless about the human touch in photography that technology will never fully replicate. The instinct, emotion, and intuition that go into capturing a moment are things that no machine can truly understand. Photography is more than just pressing a button; it's about perspective, connection, and seeing the world through unique eyes.

While technology can enhance our abilities, I think the heart of photography will always lie in the personal connection between the photographer and their subject. It's the split-second decisions, the understanding of light and mood, and the patience to wait for the right moment that give photos life. In the end, it's not the gear or the software that defines a great photo—it's the soul and story behind it.

**Embracing What Lies Ahead**

As photographers, we're part of a tradition that is constantly evolving. Every new tool and technique offers us the chance to redefine what's possible and to push the boundaries of our creativity. The future is filled with unknowns, but that's what makes it so exciting. Whether we're using the latest AI-enhanced software or sticking with classic techniques, what matters most is that we keep exploring, learning, and sharing our unique view of the world.

In the end, photography will continue to be a journey of discovery, both of the world around us and of ourselves. I look forward to seeing where technology takes us, but more than anything, I'm excited to see the stories that future photographers will capture—the moments, connections, and perspectives that will define the next generation of this beautiful art form.

**Staying True to the Craft**

While all these advancements are exciting, I think it's essential to remember that no matter how sophisticated the technology becomes, the heart of photography won't change. At the end of the day, it's about seeing the world in your own way and capturing moments that matter. Technology can enhance that process, but it can never replace the vision and passion behind the camera.

For me, the future of photography is about embracing these new tools without losing the soul of what we do. I'm excited to see where it all goes, but I'll always come back to that feeling I get when I'm out on the streets, camera in hand, waiting for the perfect moment to unfold in front of me. That thrill, that quiet anticipation as I watch life unfold through my lens, is something that no algorithm or AI can replicate. It's not about precision or perfection—it's about connection, intuition, and trust in my own eye.

Photography, at its core, is deeply personal. It's the subtle choices—the angle, the light, the timing—that bring each image to life and make it unique. No two photographers would capture the same moment in quite the same way, and that's the beauty of it. In a world where so much is automated, the human touch, with all its quirks and imperfections, becomes even more valuable. I've always believed that a good photograph should feel honest, as though you're looking through the photographer's eyes and sharing a piece of their perspective.

Looking ahead, I plan to welcome new tools and techniques into my work, but only as long as they serve the story I want to tell. For me, the magic lies in those moments that happen naturally, the ones I could never have planned. It's the unexpected glance, the fleeting light at dusk, or the shadow that falls just right—all of it reminds me why I fell in love with photography in the first place. My goal isn't to produce perfect images, but to capture moments that feel real and resonate with others on an emotional level.

So, as technology continues to evolve, I hope to stay grounded in the art itself, using each new advancement as a way to enrich my storytelling rather than replace it. The future of photography may bring changes I can't yet imagine, but one thing will always remain: that simple joy of pressing the shutter and knowing that, for a fraction of a second, I've captured something timeless.

I also think about the relationships photography builds—not just with our subjects, but with other photographers. There's an unspoken connection among photographers, a shared understanding of what it's like to chase the light, to wait in the cold or rain for that one shot, or to feel the frustration when an idea doesn't come to life as planned. Each of us brings our own perspective, shaped by our experiences and interests, but we all share that same dedication to the craft. These relationships, built on a mutual love for capturing moments, become a part of our journey.

For me, the people I meet through photography are as much a part of the story as the subjects themselves. Whether it's a fellow photographer sharing tips during a shoot or a stranger whose candid expression brings an image to life, each interaction leaves a mark. Photography is a language that goes beyond words. It's a way to connect with people, even if only for a brief moment. And those connections, no matter how fleeting, bring meaning to every shot. I think that's something no technology will ever replace—the simple, powerful exchange between the photographer and the world around them.

As I look to the future, I know there will always be new ways to create and capture images, but I hope to keep returning to these fundamentals: the curiosity that drives us, the patience to wait for the right moment, and the courage to trust our own vision. Photography, to me, will always be about the journey. It's the quiet moments of reflection as I review each shot, remembering what drew me to capture it. It's the excitement of discovering a new perspective, and the joy of knowing that my work might allow others to see the world in a different way.

So, no matter how photography evolves, I'll keep coming back to what makes it meaningful for me. I'll keep embracing the unknown, venturing into new scenes, and finding beauty in the ordinary. Because in the end, it's not just about the images we create, but the experiences, memories, and connections that photography leaves with us. And as long as I can hold a camera, I'll keep exploring, capturing, and sharing this journey—one frame at a time.

**Ethics in Photography**

Photography offers a unique way to capture the world, freezing moments in time and preserving them for future reflection. However, while the technical and creative aspects of photography are essential, understanding the ethical considerations that come with it is equally important. Being aware of these responsibilities helps photographers navigate the often delicate balance between artistic freedom and respect for privacy, dignity, and the legal rights of those they photograph.

One of the most significant ethical aspects of photography involves knowing and respecting the laws and regulations in different regions or countries. These rules can vary widely, and what is acceptable in one place may be strictly prohibited in another. For example, in some countries, photographing government buildings, military sites, or even certain cultural landmarks may be illegal without proper authorization. Similarly, laws surrounding street photography, especially when it involves photographing people, can differ significantly depending on local customs and regulations. Therefore, as a photographer, I make it a priority to always research and understand the legal framework wherever I am shooting. This not only ensures that I stay within the boundaries of the law, but it also helps me avoid situations where my work could unintentionally infringe on someone's rights or put me at odds with local authorities.

In Sweden, for example, the rules surrounding street photography are relatively permissive. It is generally allowed to take photos of individuals in public spaces without needing explicit consent, as long as the images are captured in a way that respects their dignity and safety. This means that as long as the photo does not portray the person in a negative light, put them in harm's way, or invade their privacy in a malicious or harmful manner, there is usually no issue with taking such photos. However, just because something is legally permitted doesn't necessarily mean it is ethically sound. I believe that even in places where the laws are relaxed, it's important to remain mindful of the people you're photographing. A key principle I adhere to is ensuring that I never put someone in a situation where they feel uncomfortable or exposed. For me, it's not just about following the laws but also about respecting the individuals who unknowingly become part of my images.

When photographing in cultures where I am an outsider, it becomes even more important to approach my subjects with humility and an understanding of local customs and values. Taking pictures of people from different cultures without considering the meaning it may hold for them can easily become problematic. What I see as a fascinating or beautiful shot could be intrusive or disrespectful to someone else. So when I travel and photograph in new environments, I make an effort to learn about the culture and social norms. It's about entering situations with respect and recognizing that both my presence and my camera can impact the scene I'm capturing.

Another ethical aspect of photography is how we present our images and narratives. It can be tempting to edit or frame photos in a way that heightens drama, but it's important to ask whether this truly tells an honest story. As a photographer, I feel a responsibility to show the world as it is, not just as I wish it to appear. This doesn't mean artistic expression is off-limits, but it does mean I always consider how my editing choices might shape the viewer's understanding of the subject.

For me, ethical photography also means respecting the integrity of my subjects, especially when sharing images publicly. Social media has made it easy to reach a large audience, but it also means images can spread quickly and be used in ways I can't always control. Because of this, I try to be selective about what I share and always consider how the images I publish might be perceived by others. If a photo could be misleading or damage someone's reputation, I often choose to keep it private, even if it is technically or aesthetically pleasing.

Working as a photographer isn't just about taking great pictures; it's also about understanding the responsibility we have toward the people and environments we document. Photography is a powerful tool, and with that power comes a duty to use it responsibly. I believe that by thinking ethically and showing respect for our subjects, we can create images that are not only beautiful but also meaningful and authentic. I hope that more photographers take the time to reflect on these issues and see it as part of their craft to be not only technically skilled but also ethically aware.

**interview**

I had the chance to connect with some incredible photographers whose work I truly admire, and it was an experience that really meant a lot to me. Many of them live in different countries, so meeting in person wasn't possible. Instead, I reached out to them on Instagram, hoping they'd be open to answering a few questions I've been curious about for so long. I wanted to know what fuels their creativity, how they face and overcome challenges, and their thoughts on where photography is headed.

Their responses genuinely moved me. Even though we were miles apart, their stories and advice felt close and personal, like having a conversation with a mentor. Hearing how they navigate the same ups and downs I face in my own journey was not only inspiring but also gave me fresh perspectives on my work and my approach to photography.

I'm thrilled to be able to share these interviews with you. I hope their words inspire you as much as they did me and remind you, as they did for me, of the incredible community we have in photography—even when we're separated by distance.

# Liv

Liv is an incredibly talented photographer with many years of experience in the industry. Her expertise and creative eye have made her stand out, allowing her to capture unique and powerful moments through her lens. With a deep understanding of photography and a passion for her craft, Liv continues to inspire and impress with her exceptional work.

**1. What inspired you to pursue photography, and how did you get started?**

In high school, during one of the darkest times in my adolescence, I found solace in the darkroom and film photography. It became a way for me to express how I was feeling through the art I created and developed. As technology advanced, I transitioned to digital photography, and my life hasn't been the same since. Life is full of beauty and wonder, but so many people miss it. I love bringing that beauty to the forefront and showing others that it can be found in anything.

**2. How would you describe your photography style, and has it evolved over time?**

I'm a nature photographer at heart , but I also love street, candid, and lifestyle photography—and I do equine photography as well! Over time, my style has shifted from capturing conventional beauty to focusing on things I find beautiful, like bugs, that others might overlook.

**3. Can you share a memorable moment or experience you've had while photographing?**

I worked as a school photographer for a while, and seeing kids light up with confidence after viewing their photos was always the highlight for me. It was such a rewarding experience.

**4. What are some challenges you've faced as a photographer, and how did you overcome them?**

The biggest challenge I faced was when I tried to monetize my photography. I'm in it for the art, not the money. To overcome this, I stepped back and refocused on photographing what truly brings me joy.

**5. How do you stay creative and find inspiration for new projects or shoots?**

Every day, there's something new to see. If you feel like you're running out of things to photograph, you're probably not looking hard enough!

**6. What advice would you give to someone just starting out in photography?**

Keep going, even if it's just for you. It's worth it.

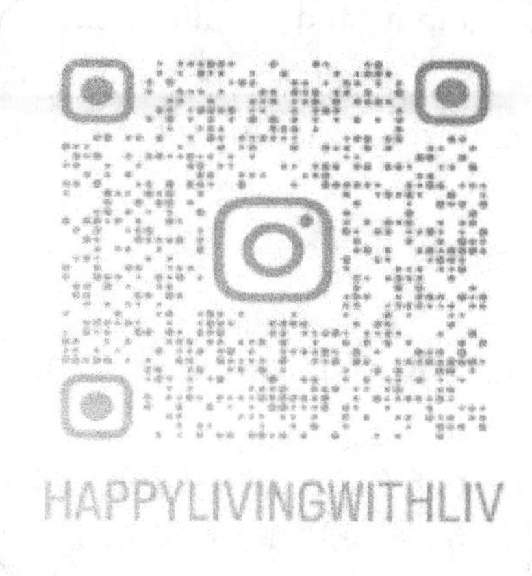

# Nickolas

Nikolas Milbredt is an incredibly talented photographer, known for his sharp eye and ability to capture breathtaking, moments. His unique style and creative vision consistently distinguish his work, making him a standout in the photography world.

**1. What inspired you to pursue photography, and how did you get started?**

Photography means to me to keep a moment and let the people see through my eyes. I started with one of the first digital cameras. Bad picture quality, but good to learn some basic features like framing.

**2. How would you describe your photography style, and hat evolved over time?**

It depends. On weddings, I prefer a bright but nuteral look; there isn't often so much time to try out.

Yes, it's evolved. There is a picture in my mind, and I know how to become real.

**3. Can you share a memorable moment or experience you've had while photographing?**

It's hard to decide. There was a young couple who ordered a photobook of their wedding. So I made one and sent it to them. Later, the bride called me in tears and ordered three more because she wanted to share it with her family

**4. What are some challanges you've faced as a photographer, and how did you overcome them?**

Setting a price tag on my work was what I struggled with.

On one hand, I want the best results for me and my clients, but on the other, I don't want to be underpaid. A good start is to look for other photographers with years of experience.

**5. How do you stay creative and find inspiration for new projects or shoots?**

There are many ways for inspiring. An easy way is social media. To stay creative, it helps a lot to have various jobs.

**6. What advice would you give to someone just starting out in photography?**

At first, don't invest in expensive equipment. Take your phone or used cam and learn the basics.

# Aras

Aras is a highly skilled Swedish photographer known for his remarkable talent in capturing stunning visuals. His photography showcases a deep understanding of composition, lighting, and timing, allowing him to bring out the beauty in both everyday moments and extraordinary scenes.

**1. Can you tell us about how you got into photography? what inspired you to take up the camera?**

My photography journey started about 25 years ago! I was always the one who brought a small camera to various events, and my interest in photography just grew bigger and bigger over the years! I started photographing at a time when there were no mobile phones with cameras, so I was really appreciated since I was the one capturing the moments! Making people happy through images is what inspires me to pick up the camera!

**2. What type of photography do you prefer to work with, and why?**

I've always loved portrait and detail photography! Working with people is challenging and puts a bit of pressure on you, which makes it an exciting challenge for the photographer!

**3. What do you think is the most important element in a photo?**

The most important element in a photo for me is the lighting! For me, it's all about the time of day and the weather! The angle of the shot and perspective are also things I consider important!

**4. How would you describe your style as a photographer?**

My photography style varies a bit, but it's mostly urban/street. I love shooting on rainy days and highlighting details like bicycles, lamps, benches, etc.

**5. Can you share a memorable photography experience or a project that was very important to you?**

Hmm, a day I will definitely remember is when I was at a track photographing motorcycles. I've always loved motorcycles, and being there in person to take photos really made my day!

**6. What equipment do you use the most and how has it affected your work?**

I've used a variety of cameras, including Pentax, Nikon, and Canon, but I eventually settled on Sony! Currently, I use a Sony a7iii with three different Sigma lenses: 24-70mm f/2.8, 85mm f/1.4, and 105mm f/1.4. I find that the selection and price make Sony's system the best option to go with!

G83.VISUALS

**Closing Remarks: A Heartfelt Thank You for Being Part of This Journey**

As I reach the final pages of this book, I want to take a moment to share my deepest gratitude with you, the reader. Thank you for embarking on this journey with me, for investing your time and curiosity to explore these words and images. It truly means the world to me that you chose to be here, taking this journey not just through the lens of a camera but also through my experiences, reflections, and growth as a photographer. It's an honor to share this part of myself with you, and I hope that something within these pages has resonated with your own journey and passions.

Photography, for me, is so much more than a hobby; it's a way of seeing, feeling, and understanding life. It's been my companion in moments of solitude, my means of expression when words fell short, and my lens to view the world with a sense of wonder. Every time I press the shutter, it feels as though I'm freezing a part of myself within that image—a fragment of my soul, my thoughts, my connection to that specific moment. Through this craft, I've learned to find beauty in the mundane, to uncover magic in the ordinary, and to see the world with eyes that are always open to the quiet, hidden stories waiting to be told. My hope is that my experiences might have sparked something within you too—a touch of inspiration, encouragement, or maybe even a gentle push as you set out on your own photographic journey.

As you set foot on your own path, remember that every photograph is an opportunity to tell a story uniquely your own, and each of those stories deserves to be captured. There is beauty all around us, often where we least expect it. I encourage you to keep your heart and mind open, to embrace the unexpected, and to cherish those fleeting, quiet moments that resonate with your spirit. Don't be afraid to explore beyond what you know; those moments of experimentation, of stepping outside your comfort zone, are where you'll begin to find your true voice as a photographer. Your unique perspective holds power, and your experiences shape the way you capture the world.

Photography has taught me that this journey isn't just about freezing what we see; it's about connecting deeply with our surroundings. Each time I bring the camera to my eye, I feel as though I'm not only observing but truly experiencing life in a profound way. Through photography, I hope you too find this sense of connection—both to the world around you and to yourself.

Of course, this path isn't always easy; it comes with its share of challenges and uncertainties. There will be days when things don't align, when the light falls flat, or when the image in your mind doesn't translate to the frame. But I promise you, this journey is rich with discovery and personal growth. Each time you pick up your camera, you have the chance to see the world from a unique angle, to connect with it in a way that's wholly yours. I wish you joy in the process, courage to push your creative boundaries, and a deep sense of satisfaction with each photo you take. May you find endless inspiration in the people you meet, the stories that unfold before your lens, and the beauty of the world in all its forms.

And if there's one thing I want to remind you of, it's that making mistakes is not only okay—it's essential. Some of the most valuable lessons I've learned have come from moments of trial and error. Photography, like life, is a continuous experiment. Embrace those missteps, allow them to shape you, and let them bring you closer to becoming the photographer you're meant to be. Every slip, every unexpected outcome is a step forward, an opportunity to grow, and a moment that brings you closer to your authentic vision.

Thank you, truly, for being here and for being part of my journey. Knowing that you've walked through these pages with me, sharing in these reflections, brings a sense of connection that's difficult to put into words. I'm genuinely excited to see the stories you'll capture through your own lens. Remember, each click of the shutter is a chance to capture a feeling, a fleeting moment, a story that's uniquely yours.

So, happy shooting. May your journey as a photographer be as fulfilling and enriching as the images you capture. Together, let's celebrate the art of photography and the beautiful, personal stories each of us contributes to it. May your camera continue to be your companion in uncovering life's beauty and wonder, guiding you to capture each frame with heart and intention. Here's to your journey, one meaningful shot at a time.